Thank you for your purch
I hope my coloring book inspires and brings you joy.
I appreciate your support! It means the world to me.

(f) Hristina Bashevski

(o) hristina_prints

GW01454338

THIS COLORING BOOK BELONGS TO

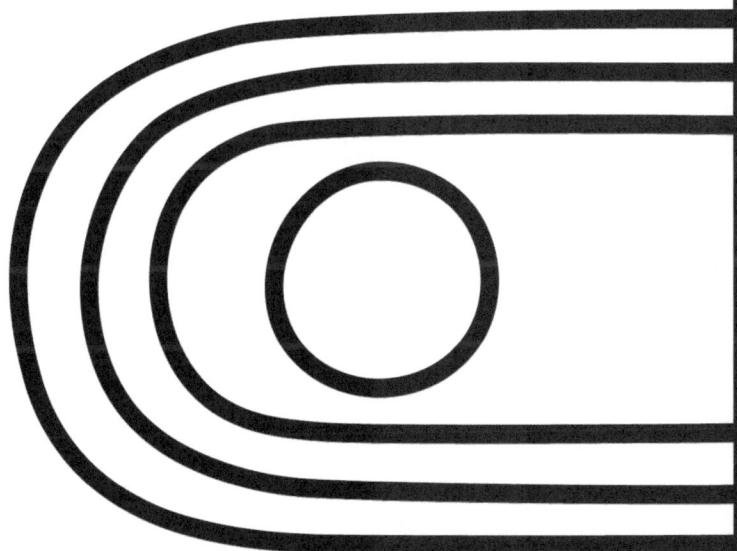

....

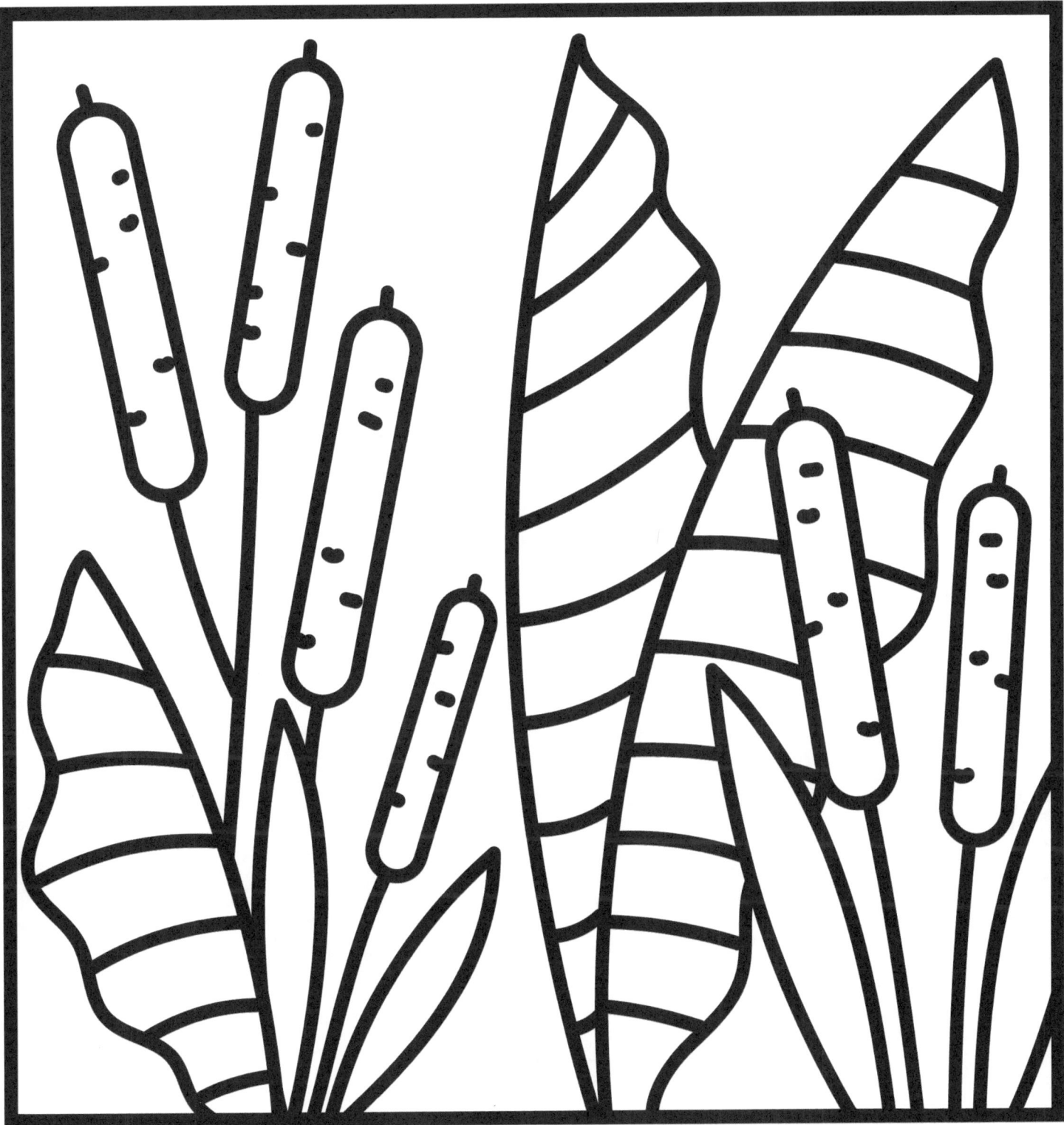

Made in United States
Troutdale, OR
05/11/2024